ACCIDENT DANCING

KEATON HENSON

·

ACCIDENT DANCING

FABER *ff* MUSIC

First published in 2020 by Faber Music Ltd.
Bloomsbury House
74–77 Great Russell Street
London WC1B 3DA

Cover and book design by Keaton Henson
Edited and typeset by Hamish Ironside
Printed and bound in Turkey by Imago

ISBN: 0-571-54179-8
EAN: 978-0-571-54179-9

To buy Faber Music publications or to find out about the full range of titles available
please contact your local retailer or Faber Music sales enquiries:

Faber Music Limited, Burnt Mill, Elizabeth Way, Harlow, CM20 2HX, England
Tel: +44 (0) 1279 82 89 82
fabermusic.com

Contents

Good Morning

Hello there breather
take pause if you will
close your weary eyes
and feel the air around you like a morning mist
wash your face with my hands
I am your dishcloth
I will lie on broken thoughts for you
if you promise to cry when I leave here
touch the pages of this book and think of all the arms that made it
that it was once trees,
made mush and pressed hard enough to print on
hold that thought gently as you read
as though I know what I'm talking about
I do not
I am a musician
who can guitar-string just about a book's worth of words together
until they fall apart like cooked wood
welcome to my wordlessness
I can write big if I want to

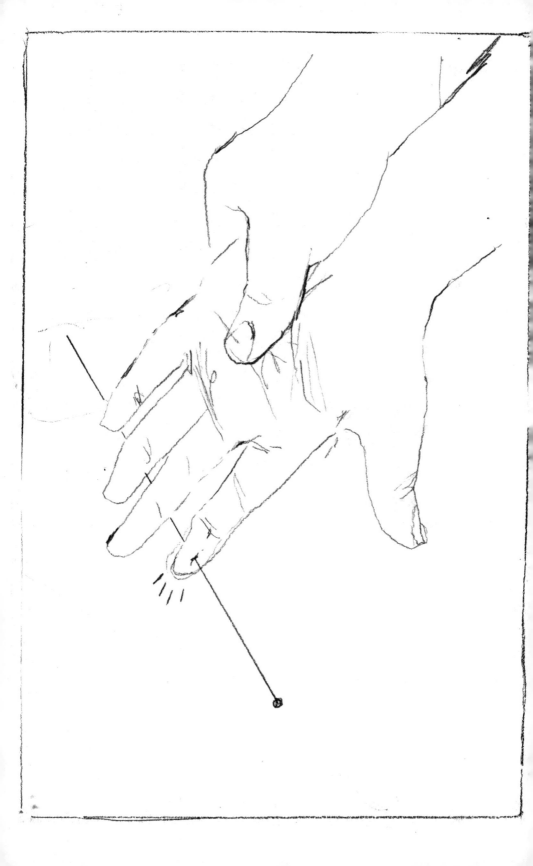

I
The Newborn Song

Notes on My Birth

O' birth canal
I don't much like the look of you
away the sound of voices
cut me out I fucking dare you

The Doomsday Kid

I was known as the Doomsday Kid.
Every sound I heard was a murder scene.

Before I knew many words at all,
I knew all the words for frightening

and would ask my parents,
as though resigned to the helplessness,

what the terrifying sound was
every time something was dropped.

The shed at the bottom of the garden
held such horrendous things,

and on Monday mornings
the rubbish truck made a nightmarish sound

as it woke me from mostly nightmares,
to an unnerving room, full of teddy bears' menacing faces.

Every second that someone was late arriving
was another second they were almost, definitely,

certainly pinned to a tree by a car,
like a moth in its casing.

And every common cold
was a fatal disease

gone undiagnosed as they fed me hot soup
as though I would soon recover.

The fools.

Halloweenboy and the Something Near

As a child I used to love cartoons about skeletons and ghosts,
I think it was the way they made the death go soft,
the round edges and primary hues of the sky,
and the way they would add in the moon
like a drop of cream in an ocean of blue
gone dreamy
all bony eyed and creepy.

Halloween was my favourite day of the year;
the kids round here,
suddenly bloody, sheet-covered,
just like me for the rest of it.
No longer was I the weird kid drawing ghouls
on the back of notepaper,
hearing the clicking of bones,
I was one of the rest, trick or treating with,
perhaps, more gusto than most,
but the sight of the back of a ghost
would be all that I needed
to feel less creepy
and like the dark stuff was the best stuff
to the rest of them too.

I used to draw car wrecks
with the ghosts of families floating wispy out the windows
I didn't know that was a pain that people were feeling
until I met two boys
who lost their mother
when a drunk came out of nowhere one night
and took away their human.
I stopped drawing car wrecks from then on,
but still drew sheet ghosts
and thought of the Mary Celeste

the years gone by put a filter between us
and made all the missing crew go silhouette
I liked them better there.

I loved anything that moaned like ghouls in the night-time
the stags in the park nearby groaning lustful calls made me think
of hulking things with red eyes
making headway through treetops to eat me up
the fear was all trickly down my spine
like something you're not meant let yourself feel.

I wore the uniform I needed
all black everything with boots made to keep you from floating away
and coats that hide your ankles
and catch the breeze
like thin skin wings
if it weren't for those boots, good grief
I'd bat-fly to bell towers easy.

I trod that Edward Gorey,
Gustav Doré, Saint-Saëns, Poe road, gleefully,
drank up stories greedily
lived in Ray Bradbury autumns
crunching cold leaves and hearing witches in the trees.
Let summer pass by like an off day,
waiting for a ghost white winter to bring me some cold
and the whistle of wind in the branches,
and almost blue evenings, where the birds are too cold to sing
so the crows do the talking,
Corvidae mornings,
lunch in that graveyard
starved of the sun.

At thirty years old, from my own to hotel to hospital rooms
I still draw sheet ghosts and vampires,
I worry less about my line-work these days,
make the arms longer than they need to be,
they float across the world I see,
they make me feel less lonely

and that hope lies,
at the end of a life,
in a deep grave,
for anyone who loves skeletons
and coffin lids
and creeping out the normals.

Hiding Places

There was a space at school
between the gym and the science building
where they stored goalposts and plastic cones
exactly the width of a human
where I would spend playtimes.

Like a pre-teen cave diver
I would crawl through
far enough in that the dark shrouded me completely
covering my navy blue uniform with thick grey dust
and close my eyes
to that inexplicable sound of the playground
as if every child alive, as soon as the bell rang
began screaming wordlessly
and flapping like geese.

So in love was I
with the loneliness
so desperate for a womb
that I could ignore the vast irony
of my sanctuary being provided
by fucking sports equipment
of all things.

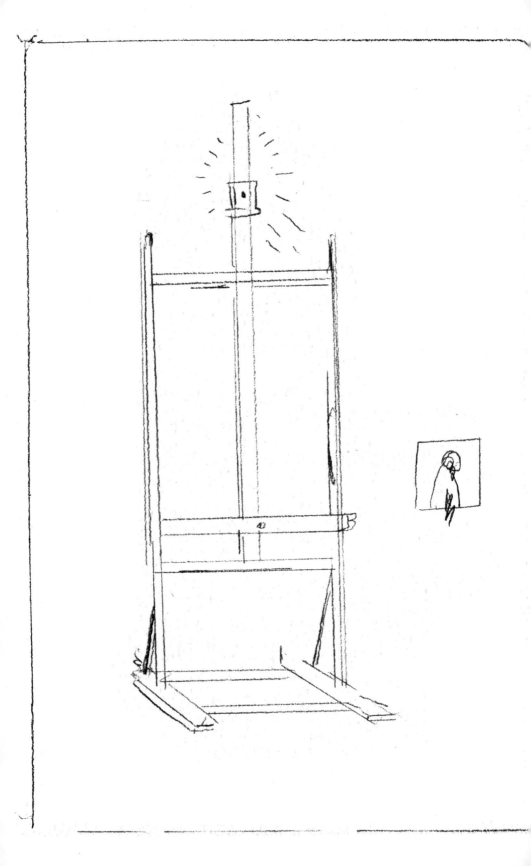

II
The Growing Still

Self-Portraits

I used to paint self-portraits
wearing band T-shirts
like a second skin,
several dense layers
of who I wanted to be seen to be.

Drawing oneself at all
seems, at once, like a sick thing to do,
and the obvious first step
in learning to realise pain,
so I draw mine
with exaggerated lines
to distract the eye from agony.

Just think of me as a superhero for loneliness.
Because I don't wear my disease like jewellery
and wait for someone to notice,
I wear it like a mask
and hope no one sees all the human behind it.

Christmas trees dumped by the roadside are we;
corpses of gaiety,
grave sites of joy,
two separate paintings
hung side by side in a hallway
arguing over whose frame is more suited to their hues
and how much better their likenesses are.

There's a picture of Jesus
(or that European, shampoo advert guy they all seem to paint)
above the bed of an elderly woman
waiting to welcome her home.

Above mine is 'The Raven', by Doré,
telling me home isn't all that there is,
that we're falling,
dying,
and talking to birds.

So paint yourself if you like
in bright colours
with better hair,
I'll be over there
erasing self-portraits,
burning my own records,
and scratching my name off the trees.

The Stick-Up

Don't be so ashamed of us,
we were young,
that wide-eyed, loose-lipped, chemical-imbalance kind of young,
diving for reasons to get out of bed,
and failing to find any
other than getting others into them.
Being me
I took the train to disorder,
woke up past the station
and crawled back to your door.

At seventeen, her and I both felt the world turn round,
we found each other's shadows in the night-time;
I was a dark spot on an old photograph,
she was a shining beam of brilliant light, with colour in its lines.
You wouldn't want to get too close though Charlie,
she might well just burn you alive.

We had that 'don't talk or you might wake it' love,
that 'don't move or you might break it' love,
the sting of something new still in our eyes,
the blood of the schoolchildren we'd left behind
still slick on our shaking hands.

We had that 'kill Paris on the staircase' love,
without blinking,
that 'come with me I'm leaving',
'as long as I'm breathing',
'home is where your feet stand' love,
young love
gone mouldy in the sun,
by now, most probably dried to something
even the birds won't pick.

I still wonder sometimes how our paths would have wandered,
how wide our arms would have grown
with each other in between them.

I held up the accident express
to steal you the plans for disaster,
robbed a bank with your love stuck under my coat.
We were a getaway car from juvenescence,
carried by drunken relatives
down a road that was always going to end.
So we tore ahead
looking for our exit signs,
pretending we were leaving together.

I was the hero of our story,
the best,
when it came to casting eggshells across your path
so you had something to step on
besides my neck
and every tall story I told.

I wrote all those songs
just to have something to remember you by.
I once fell asleep on your sidewalk
so I wouldn't have to leave your street.
I wrote your name on record covers
so people would know we were worth something.
I held on for dear life,
until like Santa Claus and easy lives
we just stopped believing in us.

The Richmond Triptych

There is a railway bridge in Richmond
under which I have imagined
all the creatures not in existence
waiting to eat me up.
Its green mossy brickwork
arching like a frightened cat,
with unkept grass clawing up the walls
and swallowing my walking shoes
as I strolled to take my mind off things.

There is a riverside path
with a stream beside it,
which flanks you with water;
the confident Thames on one side
carrying boats and their rust to the city,
and an algae'd meander
shyly housing the birds on the other,
softly singing the water's song,
when you sit still enough to hear it.

There is a view from the top of the hill,
right of 'the good one', the throng,
where the rooftops look like circuit boards
and the lights at night glimmer, sugary in the dark,
with worn benches
in memory of dead lovers,
the occasional sparrow
and the cold wind of London
whipping at your knees.

Cemetery Waltz

We skim stones on the graves of once great men
falling sideways over mildewed cemetery soil
our feet, bare, heel cold with rushing breeze
stroking at hanging boughs
bending humbly to the mossy stones.

This strange course of bewildered transience,
the ever-eternal fairground gone
with old-ride footprints, dead grass in perfect circles
a dream of what once lived and sang
with spun sugar on its hoary breath.

The most overgrown and forgotten resting place endears us the most
the unflowered, moss grown, unwanted child of a grave
the lonely churchyard orphan, with cracks along its face.

Loping echoes of once-was-people
turning their backs to your questioning hands
with humble sinking they retreat earthward shrieking
'I don't need your grief, leave me to moulder'.

Long grass brushes our ankles
fingers from underworlds, reaching homeward
like those at home, stroking the faces on family photographs
thinking of what was and won't be again.
Half sick with wonder we read and sing church bells
whistle the sound of crows in winter trees
read gravestones like novels
smiling at old fashioned names
and sink, softly to the mossy ground.

The old gates creak closed
so we sit
dancelike in the somewhere
ready for coffee and the fireplace.

Father's Day

My father's greatest role
was the voice of the Ninja Turtle hand puppet
that would read me bedtime stories
skipping past the scary parts
until I laughed myself to sleep.

My father's greatest role
was the diligent horse
upon whose broad shoulders
I rode through the park
with my tiny hands holding fast
to his scratchy throat
unshaved in the morning.

My father's greatest role
was the head of the table
the King Arthur of loud actors
holding court
and, depending on the company,
a small cigar
which smelled to my ten-year-old nose
like late nights,
and old stories,
we'd all heard a million times
but still found charming.

My father's greatest role
was the unabandoned child
whose own father had not let down
and for whom boarding school
had done only good
and taught to take the cold.

The thick-skinned
tough breaks
drinking man

My father's greatest role
was the man who wasn't frightened
of the weight of failure
perceived on his back
unafraid of the sickness he grew
when I was fourteen
that dragged him, kicking and screaming from the stage
and into the TV room.

The man who laughed through surgeries
and made deathbed jokes.

Though he was never a method actor
and I know
when the audience left
and he was alone
in the dressing room of life
the character fell from his shoulders
and he held tears to his sinking chest
no more the uncrying
comedian's son
just a frightened man
in a darkening room
without his winning smile.

III
The Newcomer

Green

Hello friend.
You're too cool,
I wish I was you,
the goddess of talking to strangers,
the deepest confessional nights,
the wishmaker,
stare giver,
genuine, head-back, laugher at friends,
name-dropper with no weight behind them and no gloat meant.

And I: quick 'brag-so-they-don't-know-me' dealer
vendor of sour words and uncomfortable jokes that don't land.
Death mentioner,
Too honest at the wrong moments fast-talker,
trying too hard at parties,
desperate to pull flesh from conversations
about what the fuck I've been doing for five selfish years,
thinking about dying mostly,
begging for mercy.

Sitting across from you at dinner, my mouth open wide
hoping to catch your eloquence like the common cold in winter.
Holy endless hell friend, how did you do that,
speak to fellow humans without tripping so far over your tongue
that your doubts get cut off at the taste buds?

I speak like these words are written,
too fast, with no regular form, and mostly to make myself look clever
you speak like a fountain,

like a friend,

like Rimbaud shaking hands with a ghost.

To the Sparrowhawk on the Airport Runway

As I prepare for the certain doom
of this aeroplane's take-off

through the oval window I watch you
hanging static in the sky

as if pinned to a painted backdrop
before suddenly swooping

in elegant arcs
above the few shrubs in the concrete grey.

Your grace and aeriform beauty
such avian talent

as if,
while I adjust my seatbelt,

I needed any further reminding
that I'm not supposed to fly.

Los Angeles Nocturne

morning ext.

You walk down the strange-treed familiar movie scene avenues,
to Larchmont,
to coffee,
to that one magazine on the stand with your face in it,
which you buy as you would something shameful
and then walk away like a thief.

It all looks so normal this way,
it all looks mythical that,
facing the formidable movie backdrop Hollywood sign
mounted on a hillside
whispering calmly
'this is not real
you do not belong here, you are far too human'.

The paving stones are hot enough to kill all imagined diseases
and turn spat chewing gum to rock,
or small statues,
if you're pretentious enough to see them thus,
which most of us living here are.
A haven of high thinking,
the land of 'this means more'.

You crawl back through the once-was-desert
to the sanctuary of air conditioning and ants.
The fridge is stocked with bottled water
and things that taste like pizza that aren't pizza.
The bed is stocked with close heat
and the stuck dreams of passing musicians.
It smells like desert wood and laundry detergent

That old adage:
how many statues of Buddha in a rental apartment
is too many statues of Buddha in a rental apartment?

You listen to the semi-famous comedian living next door
making un-comedic phone calls to loved ones back home,
and when his face appears on TV, you mute it
and imagine the laughs he gets on screen
are for the lonely declarations he utters
muffled through the wall.

You smoke softly in the calm of can't-sleep midnights
and watch the palm trees wave gentle against the still pink sky,
the cool concrete against your bare feet
makes the heat of the air like floating,
it's like living in a record cover
for an album you've never heard but know you'll like.
You listen to Joni until you fall asleep or run out of cigarettes.
'California I'm coming home'.
You dream of heaven as a landfill,
and kissing sunset pigs.

You are clearly not, but apparently cool,
apparently welcome, definitely lost.
You are on Windsor,
the other end of the avenue looks like cartoon heaven's-gates
but it's only Paramount,
same thing,
same reassuring concrete, stained by heat and gas fumes
aware it's got a way to go.

You get into cars with new friends and drive up to greener land,
though green like a miniature golf course,
not green like the forests of home,
hot green, unfilled with creatures,
not an aged oak in sight.
And scattered with glass houses
full of people who throw rocks like they're Band-Aids
and swimming pools no one will use.

You laugh at well-told jokes and hold onto that backseat handle,
gripping it as you turn up steep boulevards,
pretending you're in control of the car.
'Good grief, to be in control of something' you think.

You arrive at houses and walk into parties
where people drip over expensive rattan furniture,
and discuss screenplays and recording studios
as though they were holy texts and ancient temples.
The fire-pit's beams flutter light on the laughing faces
of people you feel like you've seen before
'where are you staying?' they say
'in that house that belongs to those people,
who manage that band' you say, 'near Lucy's el adobe' you say,
'how did you ever make it up here alive?' they say,
'I'm not sure that I did' you say.

morning int.

At A&R lunches you stare too long at waitresses
who look like the covers of magazines,
and eat foods that feel like cheating
and nod politely at the conversations about social media stats
and forget to tip,
that never made sense to your English hands.

You find the ones who mean it.
With fellow 'outsiders' comes the uncity smell,
'it's Jasmine' they all tell you,
'where?' you ask,
'everywhere' apparently.
You walk through low-slung adobe house labyrinths,
but always emerge somewhere high,
looking down on the city that's better than you,

you've made it,
you are here,
you are such a fucking human.

An Evening on a Porch on North Windsor Blvd

The sky is an upside-down swimming pool.
Pink hues from neon tubes
spraying words along boulevards blue.
Joni sings 'A Case of You', across a kitchen floor,
which I haven't cleaned this week
so is sticky like a liquor store counter.

The air is like warm water,
which makes it feel like you're swimming sitting down,
if the perfect cold of the concrete steps
weren't such a home for your feet,
bare and tingling on the morning-cool stone.

'I live in a box of paint.'

It is 3 a.m. and you have given up trying to sleep,
who could possibly sleep when California
plays its song outside your door?
You try to think of the last time you felt so much
and can only think of people.

The cigarette pressed between your sleepless, dry lips
sends its twisting grey into the world.
It is quiet enough to imagine
that you can hear one thousand American humans
turning in their beds,
dreaming of acting jobs and record deals
and paying for their children's healthcare.

You think of all the songs you have to sing
and how much there is to decide on
and a smile plays gentle across your cheek.
You are surrounded
by people from the posters on your teenage walls

you are the nothing man,
an Englander,
who has snuck in under the guise of an artist with something to say,
and you're going to inhale fully and take in every note damn it
before you're surely found out
and ejected from the sunshine,
back to the grey disowned.

The palm trees make the sound of a distant sea,
their height makes them sway like giants in a trance,
the leaves wave 'good evening' to aeroplanes
as a half-drunk in chinos walks past in a daze,
he doesn't notice you.

You are imaginary,
they never let you in,
you are not really here,
on a porch,
off of Melrose,
pressing play on Joni Mitchell,
for the third time in a row.

Soundcheck

It surprises most who know me
to hear that I loved soundcheck
like a dip in a pool
or a winter walk
and that for that one hour
I was comfortable
like Christmas day
with my parents.

I actually miss
the empty auditorium
the gaping maw of the soon to come
an echo of technicians
running cables
from the back of the room
and shouting to stage
in a language depending
on the country we are in.

The quiet in-between
and the thousands of seats
ardently empty
waiting for humans
but for now, reassuring me
'don't worry kid
it's just soundcheck
make yourself at home'.

Stepping over wires
and trying out my hands
on new pianos
freshly tuned
with novel resonations
and brightly polished surfaces
unburdened by two hundred dusty books
and tea mugs
stacked atop them
like the one I have at home.

Jumping down
to walk the aisle
and pick a seat, any seat
where I can sit
with the houselights up
watching the spectacle
of an empty stage
and hearing the overture
of occasional feedback
and operatic microphone checks
but mostly an enormous room
quite deserted.

So safe did I feel
that I have laid on the stage
like a kid gone camping
staring at the stars
and looked through
the canopy of rigging
twenty feet above
where nothing moves
but a light-cable
swaying gently
in the draught.

Running back and forth
between green room
and the wings
where my fellow musicians
tune their tools
like axes before beheadings
until they're ready
for me to plug in and test monitors,
in other words
a chance to do the thing I love
in a space most people never see
without anyone watching.

The Blind Spot

This is where I live

deep in the blind spot

deprived of the real things

hunting for my most inspiring life

like a Cheshire Cat in a cardinal-sin school

looking for ways to get out

but hoping not to find one.

I live here

left of the centre

off balance

reasoning with murderers

selling knives to serial killers

looking for my best self

in a pile of dead bodies with crooked pasts

wondering why my hands come out bloody

and where all my fingernails went

(oh right I picked them off)

I live in hope though

that one day I'll sink that buoyant knowledge

that a hospital bed lies in wait for every living soul

to soak up what's left of you

but as it currently stands

this is where I live

in an ever changing now

with my head leaking poems

my throat shedding songs

and my hands letting paintings escape them

without a thought of whether anybody cares

what these snapped bones have to say

about where they are currently living

but if anyone was wondering

it is here

somewhat loving

deep in the safe of the blind spot

IV
The Warhorse

Tidy Up Time

I am walking dry through the pink haze of a London sunset
as the last dregs of daylight glitter the office blocks
and cast long commuter shadows on filth-grey paving stones.

On certain evenings
like this
the city puts air between your feet and the ground
and becomes
all at once
all wonderful.

Where earlier the crowded bodies boiled your rushing blood
they now seem like family
or birds, in a cloud-streaked sky
parading the end of the day
and each passing footstep
makes a thrum that scores the skyline.

From Waterloo Bridge, every song lyric cliché comes to life
the lovers in arms
the finished for the day
and the just starting night shifts
all mix like paint
and I am so happy to see them
swirling the drain.

But not nearly as happy as I am
to watch the river
soberly pass beneath our aching feet
diamonds in its waveturns
and the mud, and sewage, and shopping trolleys
temporarily glimmering in the setting sun.

I can smell the familiar air
of river shores, train sweat
and surely germ-ridden hot street-side nuts
and hear the worn soles of work shoes
Everything people
ready for sleep.

Follow
    Orders

Spit me out
Tell me you love me
Take it back
Take my arms
Make them applaud my countless wrongdoings
Save me
Abrade me
Heat up dinner
Throw it out of a closed window
Defenestrate my loneliness
Tell me it's nearly over
Tell me we aren't all dying
Kill me I fucking dare you
Cut it out
Cut my hair with a blunt knife god damn
Damn me
Mean what you say
Say I didn't warn you
Say it all over again
Say it's all over again
Make it rhyme
Make it happier
Make it 140
Write a chorus
Add drums
Adhere
Hear me out
Out me
Kick at my heels
Heal me from laughter
Laugh at my longing
Wolf my door like you mean it
Mean it when you say it

Send me flowers
Send me packing
Pack my bags
Bag my corpses
Corpse when you're meant to be silent
Silence the alarm
Empty the register
Call the police
Take me upstairs
Stare too long
Mother me
Brother me
Lover me
Leave
Hold my hand
Hold me back
Hold.

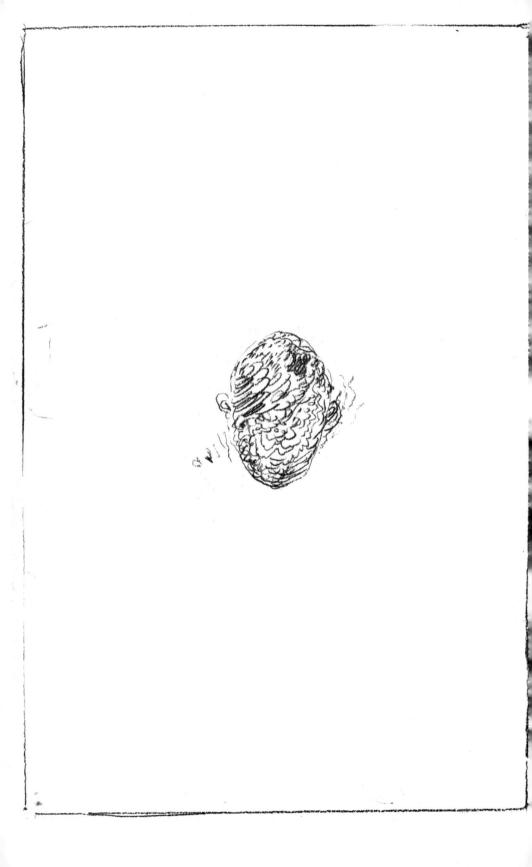

The Masochist

Some days,
tired of keeping busy,
I carve the nails from my fingers.
Whittle them from my very hands,
and collate them in piles on my bedside.

Some long afternoons,
I take the teeth from my head,
one by one, with no thought
for the nerves that attach them,
and make toy soldiers of my molars just because.

I get bored sometimes,
and peel off my tired eyelids
so I can make my fingers blink
and run the lashes softly
across the back of my neck.

And occasionally
I crack open my ribs,
to pick at the tender organs
exposed underneath,
and always wonder
at how unlike the cartoon version
the human heart is
and can totally see
how we one day looked
at that gruesome thing
and felt it should represent love.

Mantra

feel unloved.

google yourself.

feel worse.

repeat.

The Hobo's Song

'Hell I'll bleed for you, you ask me to'
he says, leaning everlonely to my side,
'I'll write the woes of my stillbirth on your arm,
you ask me to.
I'll hold open your eyes while you're dreaming
to make 'em all seem real' he says
'scratch the pain in my side into your palms,
pin down your arms,
sound the alarms,
pick at your teeth,
with my teeth,
and read you the stories
your dad skipped when you were a child,
you ask me to.
I'll fix your broken bones for you
so's you can break 'em all over again'
he says.
'I'll be the one'
he says
'to sell you songs,
remind you of wrongs,
breathe in your ardour,
tell you try harder,
tell you "there there",
make fun of your hair,
and your love for Randy Newman.
But don't you go askin' for love'
he says
'I'm only human.'

A Wedding in Calabria

We undock in Italy
from the port at Messina
car sick and tired of inside

Your dad drives
like he's testing the steering
and your mum tells him where he should have turned

The heat drives pins in my arms
the sea, though blue, brings little comfort
and the beds may as well be wood floors
(good lord)

You, are a balm to my sunsick bones
your pale skin gone shimmery in the brightness
as your intricate fingers roll cigarettes in the back of the car

We laugh about childhood driving games
you used to play with your brother
who is getting married tomorrow

Which, I can tell by your face
but can't find the reason
seems to unsettle you so

The Gioia Tauro piazza
sits like a scratched wound
stitched with a handful of plastic chairs

I sit there alone while you sleep
in the daytime like a native
or a cat

We have breakfast with in-laws
who don't speak English
but slap my back like they're uncles of mine

Your tongue speaking Italian
is like one of your best songs
you are my tour-guide

An ancient dream
a sun-bleached statue
insecure in your own stone skin

And I love you more in sunlight
than any dark London day
when we hide from the rain writing verses

We smoke and eat pastries in the dry air
and walk to your parents' rental apartment
to try and catch a glimpse of the ocean

The church is wild white
it smells of old tradition
the sinister wooden pews

And they throw water at us
with a silver utensil
as if we are on fire

I sit still
applaud politely
hold your white hand

And at the party we fall apart
you get sloppy drunk
I behave badly to spite you

Like a child who won't share his toys
I sit Byron-like in the moonlight
waiting for someone to notice

Your cousins spill drinks on me
talk loudly in my ear
as you look through me

To the horizon
where a sun sets
like a karaoke screen

And is eaten by Etna
when I wander away
till the music fades

And watch night birds
until you find me
and we slow-dance alone

In the hotel car park
watched by a tired valet
we sway like willows

Both aware it may be
a dance to our deaths
more than a waltz of love.

Aeroplanes

Darling ether
everleaving pleasure giver
I've never wanted anything more than to dream you
and wake up to see you exist
these days, come to think of it, I want nothing more
than to dream of anything at all.
I beg you
don't watch as I leave
it's too painful
have some sense
let us be
hold my things till I need them
hold my hair back as I bend
'cause creature I'm sick to the break of my bones
of watching every aeroplane passing overhead
and wondering if you are on it.
How many dreams are you breathing?
Cabin-pressured-sleep dreams
sicksweet love never held charm for the two of us
too many kisses and hearts
not enough breaking of limbs and careers
leaving the cold where they are.
And when you land
and they ask what you have to declare
tell them that though I am far away
it will all be OK
because you will come home
tell them you will come home.

Best Newcomer

Hello up-and-comer
welcome to the party
leave your coat on

I'm so glad to see you made it
what a voice you have
and what things you have to say

this is everyone else
they all mean well
don't take anyone to heart

it seems like yesterday
that I was where you are
coming in wet from the rain

with my hair over my eyes
a bottle under my arm
and a story I was sure everyone would love

when the hug of the host
felt like a cry I'd been holding in
the whole journey here

the view from the windows is decent
drink in the sky
the food is mostly free

but don't eat too much or they'll own you
don't take the host at his word
and don't take anyone too seriously

when they tell you things that sound like praise
and promises
and blame

because this is not your moment
this is a moment
and there will be others

both in and out of the spotlight
as large as a standing ovation
as small as the warm night air.

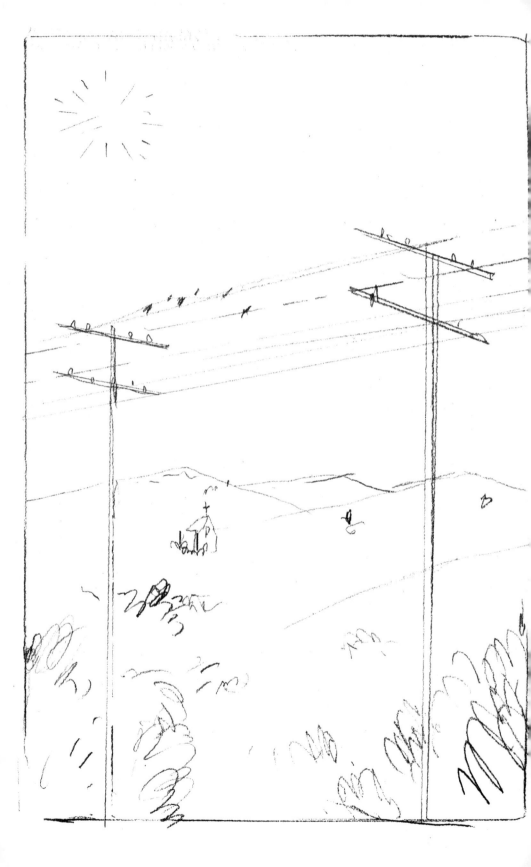

(A Desert Near) Barcelona

I watched the sun come up
in a desert near Barcelona
next to a make-believe car wreck,
with only the sound of crickets
and my own song playing far in the distance
over cheap speakers,
and the way the grass moved
made me feel like I was in a painting
which doesn't exist,
by an artist I've never heard of
but definitely like.

Performer

Performer,
you are standing naked in the parking lot of humanity
waiting for a compliment.
You'll catch your death.

Performer,
if you keep eating chunks of yourself off the bone for applause
there won't be much of you left to applaud,
let alone walk with lovingly
or hold in cold mornings when you can't get to sleep
because the world's too loud outside your door.

Performer, don't spend too much of your life howling at the moon
for being bigger than you or it might just come down here to bite you.

Every day you spend telling others about the way you live,
you lose another you could've spent living,
weaving yarns to become more than a man for so damn long
that you become less than a man, just a story.

Performer, the need to remain's got you so far removed from the –
breathing of days, that even the most experienced of overwhelmed –
nightshift, immigrant, mothers of three couldn't teach you to live in –
the now of it.

Hold close your sleeping darlings
one of these days you'll stop dreaming
get sick at the sight of your name
hate the sound of dancing shoes
and lose your voice from singing.

Performer, if you desire love so much, be kinder,
tell truths instead of tall stories, love deeper yourself.
You are welcome always in the sunlit now

but with every absent hour spent scratching 'I was here'
into an intricate tombstone of breathing,
you push yourself further away,
making the statement less and less true,
you're still welcome though dearest,
it'll just take you longer to get here.

That cold feeling, shivering to yourself, alone in the hotel room
with the sound of applause still ringing shrieks in your ears.
that's the reward for your bleeding.
You'd do better to go collect break-ups
for that hollow feeling that love existed but ate itself whole.

Performer, the ones around you speaking 'this matters'
to your open-wound ears are just hungry,
I know they made you feel warm for a spell
and they mean you no harm but need feeding.
You've spent the good part of a decade as bait,
the things you create, dangled outward like so much glittering tin,
pieces of your insides dangled limply in muddy waters,
something to catch their eyes just long enough to make them bite
but it all means so much more to you,
and that's the bit that is meaningful
hold on to your making, the biting doesn't make it so.

You get the picture performer,

I won't go on.

Art is for getting your hands dirty.
music for dancing and crying,
stories for keeping your loved ones warm and helping the time tick by.

So paint broad arcs and enjoy the feeling of a line being born,
the warm satisfaction of something suddenly existing
as a by-product
of your day spent warding off the yawning maw of meaning.

Breathe a sigh of soft relief
as the dirt of a day well spent runs in circles round the drain.
Hold close the echoes of keys as you push the typewriter
back under the desk,
stack neatly the pages and enjoy the weight of their mass.

And while you pick paint
from under your fingernails at the dinner table
smile knowingly to yourself by all means,
but then eat dinner,
and ask someone else how their day was.

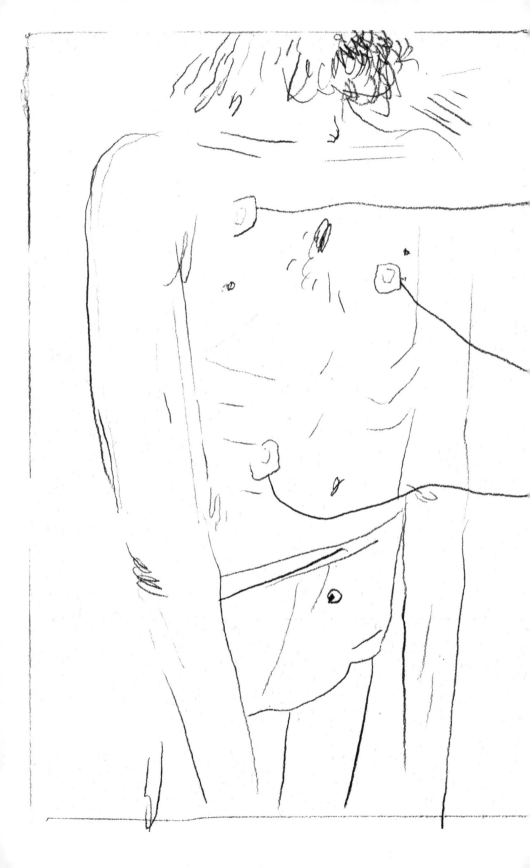

V

The Long Way Down

Andrew Wyeth in East London

Wyeth in east London
would have slammed shut his shop grate
lifted his collar to the rain
boarded the last train
and wondered why all the flustered bodies
looked like so many grieving ants
dragging their morsels to erstwhile homes
stacked on top of one another
with no real light.
He would paint his bedroom walls
and want to add trees
among the white snowstorm.
He would lie in bed at night
pretending the sirens were birdcalls.

Wyeth, tired on Ridley Road
would smack his brow with wondering
how so many creatives
lived such creative lives
while striving to keep up appearances,
beating dead horses in evenings
and every Christmas
leaving the streets of east empty
as they all fled back to Sussex
to roll their eyes at aunts.

Wyeth in Hackney would look for trees
and find sad their fettered edges
uninspired by the fences so diligently mended
by a council told their borough
was a home for artists
a melting pot of culture
when all the real culture had been thrown from the pot
diluted in the west of it

whitened like a fencepost
that had stood for years
collecting interesting marks worth painting.

Wyeth in east London
would turn his cragged face from coffee shops
and look for something wild to paint
something past buildings
pure-bred air come whispering across fields
to move that hung washing just for him
he would close his windows on weeknights
to shut out the sound of the free-jazz, dub-house club nights
and try to dream of distance
of clustered trees and long grasses in breeze, and Christina
crawling westward toward the farmhouse
the wind whistling choirs around her
the grey of old wood
the white of new snow
black tree fingers emerging from its softness
forests on horizons, leading the eye to white cliffs and wild water
the smell of salt and rot and evenings
of Chadds Ford, Cushing
Wyeth country.

In Memoriam KYG

KYG

My friend who spoke like laughter.

who sang like breathing,
left you breathless
and then told you he was worthless
before walking clean away.

He was a man who, at his lowest,
lifted you higher than you could stand,
to see over all the awful,

Played guitar like a river picks up leaves,
told stories like somebody counting a breeze,
talked like he saw the world slipping away
and dared to be friends with
me.

We would laugh in local parks,
write songs
which he would throw out,
shiver in line for shows,
secretly take ourselves seriously
when no one was looking
and talk about the state of the world.
Until I lost the strength in my arms
to drag him outside again
and lost my voice
from telling him he was worth something,
on deaf ears
and a heavy heart.

Kiran.
Yashin.
Ghanty.
My friend in a burial shroud,
We put him in the ground on a dreary day,
that English grey of half-hearted weathermen
'more of the same',
but none of us complained.

We placed him in a basket, choked back bitter tears
nodded weak hellos, some high-school reunion,
walked from ceremony to hole in the ground,
a parade of school friends, all grown up,
looking like children wearing their parents' clothes
who wanted to be back at home.
The imam sang Salat al-Janazah
and the sun came out
and we made jokes
about the few times he failed us
and how he made the day go shiny
and how long it had been.

K Y G
eventually,
too sad for days on earth,
left us alone
in June 2017
with a book
left open
by his empty frame
for the ambulance to read
entitled *Missing Out*
like we will be now
on all he was bound to be.

Joining In

I am not joining in.
Death-bound, listless, buyers of bedside tables all.
I once had more hope for us,
I once thought I might make it out alive.
I feel now the fog of my mind makes it difficult to have such faith
or write good poems
or stand up straight in the snow.

I have an apparently-ailment you see
that has stopped me from joining in.
It's as though the filter switch was flipped,
and I was left wide-eyed without wiper blades or eyelids,
staring horrified at the sun,
suddenly aware we're rotating
and that dying hangs languid over me,
its oily loose-skin hands dragging too fucking close to my head
for me to look up and see anything other than
TV static and hospital beds.

'Anxiety', the buzzing word, cannot contain every secondly scrape
of my head on the floor as I'm horse-drawn, facedown
across a landscape of inescapable beauty,
craning my neck between bumps to catch glimpses
and salting my wounds as I do
with tears of not joining in.
I'm not joining in
and made worse my journey
by the sight of others, similarly dragged,
some unclothed, some double speed
across the glimmering lands
and screaming half as much.
Or equally by those atop the steed
dressed and unharmed howling double-loud at the sunlight.

Good god, how can I sing efficiently with my tongue cut to ribbons,
my lips fat and bloodied and my brain tied with rough cord?
So I type badly, slowly,
no more satisfying crescendo of taps, as a song pours out of me
begging for air.
Nevermore originality, and the idea they haven't had,
rushing to beat the world to writing it down.
I have had the distinct privilege, and nerve,
to look at my life as something completely distinct and worthy.
Aware everyone else feels the same,
but also sure they must be wrong, surely.
I have lost, and don't feel sorry for myself
but still, I dare you to watch me burn inwardly as I'm dragged
from afterbirth to formaldehyde, facedown on jagged rocks while my –
brain chatters one hundred discouragements in several languages –
I don't speak and fucking tell me to 'take deep breaths'.

I am not joining in.

I am holding out for something better
than biting off hunks of my own tongue, trying to explain
what I'm feeling,
praying for one hour of sleep
and blazing to be more than pain.

But, as I, horse-dragged, burning, go,
occasionally it softens,
the foaming beast grows weary
and the blaze turns to embers in my bones
my neck, though aching, allows me a glance around,
and in that moment, if I can force myself to care,
force myself not to spend that time thinking
about the ordeal I have endured,
or delude myself it's over to plan some false future, and just look

at the world around me,
no matter where the sun lays in the sky,
or what the trees do with their leaves,
good grief it's beautiful,
it fills your bones to the marrow and your skull to the stem
with wonder, and relief and privilege
but, I feel the horse come restless, the fire start to grow as I gaze,
so, half revived, I can take a final breath,
glad I got to see it all,
somewhat joining in
looking forward to seeing it again someday.

Mineshaft

The canary lost consciousness hours ago
why are we still in here
can none of you see I'm a housefire
dancing my wares on a lake
made of pre-supposed symptoms
run for your lives
those that still have one

Monolith

Good morning endless. I feel as though it's definitely going to happen but might not happen now. if I try to focus on the 'might not now' I might not lose my mind so. but the fact remains that many saner than I try to remember what I cannot forget. that it's definitely going to happen but might not soon. I might have longer, if I focus on the 'might have longer' I might have longer to figure out a plan. to be OK when it does. I need to be prepared for the worst to happen, because it definitely will. I will certainly lose my life. but I can just hope to lose it before my mind. entirely at least. I'm not sure what percent I still have. I'm definitely emptier than before. but somehow feel heavier. weighed down by the growing thought that it's definitely going to happen and I don't know when. thank god I suppose, nothing to count down to. I can't keep holding on to the fact that 'I woke up' like it's a solid oak banister rail and I'm treading on rain rotten stairs. hope is something I wait for in the evenings. and cling to like wet fabric to skin, like a child to a leaving mother. but like all things clung to, it leaves me quite bereft, quite often. quite alone in the night, re-aware that it's definitely going to happen but might not tomorrow, and that tomorrow I could go to a park and drink the sky in, or paint my best woman in shades of grey until my fingers are so slick with clove oil and paint that I can't hold on to my troubles so tight. and the room smells like christmas and art class. and at the end of that full day of living I will remember that it will definitely happen but didn't today, so might not tomorrow, and fall into milky sleep. and tomorrow somehow wake up completely once more in the throes of feeling as though it will definitely happen today, and if it doesn't happen now it will almost definitely happen later. and grab at the 'almost' like a disappearing balloon string. too late we lost it son. maybe it's happening now and I don't know. I don't want to know if it's happening now. I hope to forget for just one blissful, hungry, lustful, living moment that it's able to happen at all, like when I was young and full of the arrogance of childhood. spitting at the sky. tearing at the universe, outraged at the air that something could take my father away. I long for that outrage, the injustice of youth, compared to the resignation of the over thirty. aware that life drives on and the eyes sting upon waking, and grow lines from their edges. that the spine begins to fold itself in, like it's packing up at the end of school.

no more running from sleep old man. you sit alone in the studio, supposed to be working, but vibrating with the thought that it's definitely going to happen and could happen right now. and if not now definitely later. I feel the nag of the fact that I could put the thought that it will definitely happen and could happen right now into song, or poem, or drawing. maybe then the dreadful knowledge will be worth something to me, and do something more than frighten my skin to shivers and make me shudder off my balance beam. this, I suppose, is an attempt to do so, though rather a dense and self indulgent and overly descriptive and underly interesting attempt. oh look, self loathing, how postmodern. oh look, sarcasm, how 1993, vague humour tricks me into thinking that it might not happen today, maybe today I can just be, maybe I don't have to fill every moment of it with dancing wildly, to try and shuck the fear from my back. maybe I can eat breakfast with the human I love and watch her shake the night away, and beam at the day before her, without worrying that I'll ruin it for her by the fact that it's definitely going to happen. without choking on my terror and forcing her to soothe the shiver from my bones until I'm OK and she's too tired and has to sleep. good god what was that, that was definitely something to do with the fact that it's going to happen. that must mean it's going to happen soon. I should probably head for cover, or make it happen before the world can have its way. on my terms, without pain. in a garden. but no I think I'm OK. I have strength to reason with the planets once more and decide if it's worth it to go outside. it's sunny but cold. that bones-cold with streaks of sunlight. if you lie down and the rays catch the lids of your closed eyes it feels like someone turned the lights on in your whirring skull. and you're looking out from the womb again, ready to start your life. and that it's probably not going to happen right now. so you can breathe and count and think of things you'd like to write tomorrow, like a dense and un-paragraphed mess of feeling. a mud-mire of words pulled out like a mile of intestines in some vague attempt to convey the chaos of living in your minutes. oh look, self awareness, how 'poignant'. that ends 'remember still child, it didn't happen today, today was just today, as tomorrow will be when it comes, if you can bring yourself to wake up and think it so. and that after a long night of dreaming that all will be OK, all might be OK.'

Time Machine

Every second is a time machine
that takes us from now
to after now

but it helps if you run

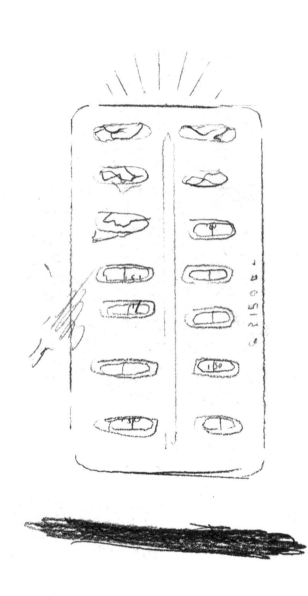

Psychiatric Hospital Blues

You arrive, bleary-eyed, shaking,
speaking in tongues and bent over for fear of the sun
admittance means it's over, you've finally lost the fight
you sign papers, dizzy, and become aware you are now a citizen
of a world that speaks in sympathetic voices
and closes its doors to keep you safe inside,
or outside safe from you.

Stiff bedsheets and the familiar smell of school cafeteria food.
'I'll eat in my room' you say
'I just need sleep'
'I just need sleep' you say
'I think I'll feel better then'
you say.
You finally eat as though it's the sea and you're drowning,
drink water like you're putting out throat fires,
sleep like it's finally safe to.
You walk, shivering, through the corridors on spongy carpets
everything soft,
lacklustre cream-coloured, hiding-god-knows-what-stained walls.
You make fast friends with the dead insects on the windowsill
and reacquaint yourself with daytime television,
antiques shows mostly.
But you earn your first laugh in four weeks upon turning it on
to a documentary about King Ludwig II
your very favourite historical lunatic
'if I'm going down I'm taking one of them down with me' you think
'poor Ludwig' you think.

'Fifteen minute obs' means your day is spent
mostly telling faces around the door that you're OK.
At night you can feel them tense cringing round the frame,
you know what they're dreading they'll see.

Awake, hot bath, water a funny colour,
'damn it how long till I feel something again'
the plastic clock says only 'I'm OK'
antiques shows,
soft carpets.
You collect paper cups
for some reason.

The meds have you walking like the world's spinning too fast for you,
maybe it is and that's the problem,
maybe you're moving too slow,
so you stumble from nurses' station to bedroom
past patients making too much noise,
and patients not making enough of it,
noticing your feet start to take on
the limping skip shuffle of madhouse blues.
'I'm hoping I don't stay too long' you sing,
like Leadbelly
caught light on melatonin slackjawed and breathing way too hard
'I'm hoping they don't make me leave' you sing.

On the better days friends visit in twos,
with cigarette packets rolled up in spare socks,
'this is normal' painted white across their welcome faces
they stay for as long as you can take it,
and leave like they're fleeing the scene.
Nobody comes when it's worse.
'your room seems OK' is the chorus
'what the fuck happened' 's the verse

At one 3 a.m., groaning night you smoke
alone in the communal area, moonlit and clouds in the night
and hear a kind of crying you haven't ever, and never want to hear again.
The sound of someone who has lost everyone, including themself.

You don't finish your cigarette that night,
you do not go for help.
The night-shift nurses do colouring in,
as there is clearly nothing more reassuring
when one has lost their senses
than the repeated sight of an adult man colouring, the fuck, in.
'Inhale, white smoke, exhale black smoke'
'Notice your thoughts' they say
'I'm sorry I think I have to go back to my room' you say
'excuse me, I just have to go back to my room'
your room is far too quiet
so you go somewhere else.

You walk sometimes, outside,
you get as far as the gates,
but it feels like there's a bungee cord of nausea,
tying your guts to the sink.
Sink down,
comfortable now,
held by the castle.
'No more group' you say, your new mantra
'no more group please' you say
'I can't bear to hear one more woe' you say
'and the ones who come in but then get to leave',
'please don't make me watch them go,' you say
'no more' you say.
How long now, you don't count.
How did today's dessert become something you stake such a care on,
how many cycles of said desserts has it been.
Friends are giving birth out there good god and I am counting teeth.
And how on turned-earth did you get to the point
where one-on-one room visits with doctors in suits that cost more
than your left arm are the highlight of your fucking week.

You begin to fear more, the grey absence
in the eyes of your fellows with every light turn of a door,
straight to the floor, go they,
with one wrong phone call from a loved one
who just can't take the not-making-sense of it anymore,
the brief sparks of interesting;
sudden crashes, lights out, loping bedroom bound,
used to the sound of the door by now,
don't even say you're OK,
they know,
or care less these days.

The broadway gang of IV-tubed eating-disordered
heron-like hallway stalkers seem to cry more than most,
different wings for different strokes,
strokes go in east and stay quiet.

Eventually the nurses come in one by one to look at your drawings
they've discovered your secret identity,
you show them like an evening, showing someone else's dawn.
'Good lord,' you think,
'if you all could have seen me before.'

You swallow pills like warm water,
step heavy,
burn your lighter to the nub,
dress more like you're sleeping,
scream inwardly, speak politely, smile,
and on one warm, courtyard, lunchtime smoke
a fellow loose-screw finds you lonely,
with as friendly a face as a face can be
filled eyelids high with Olanzapine and secondhand symptoms of doubt.
'I think I just learned to let out' you say
'good for you' she says

'I thought it would feel better' you say
'nope' she says 'feels like shit' she says
'it does' you say,
and hold that gravid silence between you
like the greatest conversation you've ever had,
and then call someone far away,
and tell them you're scared and can't hope,
you let go,
of any rope you were holding,
and fall gladly
into the buoyant mist of 'I don't know where I'm going,
but when I get there I'll write it all down' you say
and just hope that who reads it comes looking.

Orchestra Song

There was a day before I was used to it

when fifty odd people

who know their instruments better than the back of their eyelids

played my thoughts for me.

Amassed

at agreed time

and spelled out a song I'd been hearing

for two months

in the back of my head,

among thoughts of much less pleasant things

and a decent amount of confusion,

but there it was, clear as day

an orchestra song all along.

I think it's the kindest thing anyone has ever done for me.

London England

On foreign snow I hold my tongue.
I hold my tongue now,
and how heavy it feels in my mouth.
Smokeless I, leaving London,
missing it somewhat;
not holding my tongue,
the sounds of everyone living, crammed into one concrete claw.
How the rain filled its shoes and spilled over,
making rivers of its every street and dark corner
the deafening hum of the human hive,
the soft light from open-late offices,
setting fire to the rain-streaked windows of passing cars and taxis.
I held dear rehearsing orchestras, seconds away, tightening bows,
re-hearing the melodies ready for war,
the West End actors going home for the night,
sharing late-night trains with prostitutes with podcasts in their ears
and cum still drying on their ready-for-TV-day jumpers
held tightly, the thousand neon lights, buzz in harmony
a chord we've heard our whole lives
but couldn't begin to recognise.

How late the fumbling car key seekers,
caliginous gurning followers of shop-window light,
nightbus drinkers,
Kingsland Road just-trying-to get-homers,
smiling-at-girls-on-trains-
who-would-rather-be-left-alone-to-read motherfuckers,
cold-coffee-spilling late-workers,
lain-in-the-doorway-of-churches-
so-you-can-feel-somewhat-closer-to-god rough-sleepers,
deep breathers,
on Waterloo trains,
fogging the windows with musty air from still-waking lungs

and staring like the dead,
hope living its days on the opening doors,
the moment of cold on a rush hour train,
letting out the morning breath, heady in the breeze,
carried away to the country.
So lost was I, I lingered,
held on
left over
left it too late and turned against you,
my old town
turning my back to the grey
crossing my fingers and knowing
that I'll never need you again.

An Ontario Home

The white forever came today,
snowfall, silent, blank canvas, dust-sheet morning.
I went out into it gladly,
vision tunnelled by fur hood, black peripheral hug of goosedown
making the white circle of outside all the more blinding and glory.
Until, like soft focus, the trees come into being,
the branches spread out,
spindle fingered interlocking and ready to shield me from sky.

The bridge is quiet, the maintenance stalled,
allowing me to walk over the antlered water in one dry piece
I look up, to nothingness alive with the sparkling now
gulls flitting circles, the sudden moon,
their wings flashing harsh against pink snow-cloud skies
as the river brings the hopeless to lakeshores.

The baseball field, white blanket,
empty seats and creaking-in-the-wind floodlight poles,
the soft bending bleachers sat-still,
waiting to groan at the sound of the summer.
The echoes of cheering and the knock of the ball
hang listless in the air, as I walk, half-interested, past it.

Power lines, those dreams of my England childhood,
spreading languid down streets
lined with disparate wood-sided houses and skeleton trees.
The suburban crackle of near perfection
and poster-hung bedroom walls, elbow-length gardens,
tennis shoe bicycle rides and Halloweens at sundown.
'It's just how I dreamed it' says I.
'You're just in time to watch it melt' says the season.

The squeak-crunch of my feet making pathways in Ontario snow
speak with every broad step I take,

sending warnings through the trees
to every shivering creature that hides there,
and take me further away from home.

My ears burn and the wind beats at the few exposed stitches of skin,
shaking loose my thoughts of home, and death, and unreason.
The bright of outside squints my eyes,
and tears fall slowly, unnoticed down my numb cheeks
and salty upon my cracking lips
that curve up at the edges, a smile snuck soft across my narrow face.

The main-event snowflakes have ceased,
but remnants fall from the gently waving boughs above me,
points of white in agreement with the wind,
until they land without sound
and become more of the same around me.
The once sterile and seamlessly demarcated pathways
are now no different from the chaos beside them,
all snow, and rare footprints,
freedom from being told where to walk.

The smell of cold is a strangely reassuring thing,
the sting of its waking is worthy,
as much as it shivers me, burns at my face and fingers,
this walk will not kill me,
not this time.
The house is not far; its radiators and thick windows,
the heap of bed linen
and she
the warmth of her waiting.

Nervous Girl

This nervous girl seems not nervous
when she takes my soaring words in her throat
and spits them out like apple seeds,
when she carries my burdens
round her aching neck like a necklace at a ballroom.

This shy creature seems not shy when she tells me she has my back
and that I'm going to be OK when she gets here,
when the dust of Eden swarms her clothed body
and she sees it only as passing rain
to help the plants grow tall.

This anxious little thing seems not anxious
when, anxiety-bound, she talks to strangers at parties,
takes the metro in Paris to meet me,
and makes a home of Père Lachaise tombstones
as a place to read her book.

This nervous girl seems not nervous
when her small hands hold my body from shaking,
when she shouts at the sun for waking me up,
makes faces at fields of snow,
dances in the living room,
lives in the dancing room,
discovers every season,
beats at the door of madness,
and tells it to come out here and face her like a man.

When she climbs a stage to sing her failings to a talking crowd,
places her sculptures in galleries,
where people kick them over
while backing up to view the more attention-seeking works,
and shrugs to see them go.

When she talks me into failing,
picks me up from falling,
de-tunes my piano,
and tells me 'try again'.
She seems not nervous when she takes deep breaths,
when she holds up her nervous fists
to the oncoming storm and shouts back to me
'I've got you, stay behind',
all the while carrying axes to grindstones and friends across finish lines
without even breaking a sweat.
I think I like this nervous girl,
she's got guts.

Upon Waking Without You

I woke this morning hoping to grief
that you would sing one more time
down my wanting throat
that song that made me love you so.

I woke this morning with it stuck in my head
the chorus come lively to my tongue
to remind me
I have you to look forward to
every day for as long as you'll keep me around.

I woke, holding my own dead arm
pretending it was even
half the arm you are
and that its fingers held a candle
to the ones you own that run like sand
through my hair when I can't sleep.

I woke this morning without skin
open to the elements
trying to keep the dust motes
from landing on my lidless eyes
knowing that you would shield me
when you got home from work.

I awoke to the sound of birds
screaming at my window
incensed, that you could exist
and I would not drag my bones across an ocean
to be where you are
every day I'm able
until the day I'm not.

Overcome

Dwell not dearest.
Sit not in the wrongdoings of that heavenly brain,
hold not too dear the things that hurt you.
Life is fucked-rotten and gasping-beautiful in equal measures,
count both with objective wonder.

Wallow not darling.
Ask for help when needed,
talk to others when you feel you can't hold on,
but sometimes go outside
and laugh wildly at something
even if it's your own misfortune.

Take not credit for pretending you're OK,
recognise that you are OK
and just showing the world that fact.
You are able to walk, see, hear, feel, at the very least think,
what a miracle,
what an opportunity to carry on.

I have seen you smile like you're hiding a secret,
let it spread across your face,
force it if you must,
show it to others,
no matter how it undermines the foundations
of the suffering statue
that you have been building,
hoping someone will see its magnitude
and somehow come running to save you.

Dwell not my heart,
we are here for you if you need us,
but you don't,
you can save you,
I can only really say what my mother brought me up on:
that 'all is well and all is well and all things shall be well'.

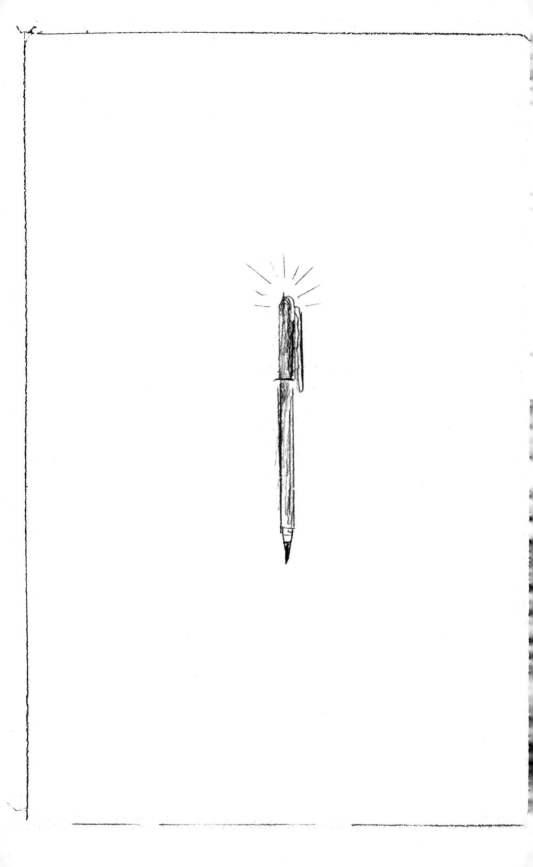

VI
The Long Way Up

Thank You Letter

This is a poem in thanks
to all the previous ones
that have given me
the duration of their creation's worth of peace.

The ones that have taken my breath away
and poured out like water,
the ones I have to wrestle to the ground
and hold between my legs while I reach for the rope,
those that are a chess game between me and my thinking self
where occasionally one of us wins
and makes something worth reading.

It is almost especially
for the ones I write throughout a tough day
that take all my energy and emotion
and remove my thoughts from unpleasant things
and then disappear once I've left them,
lost in the back of a notebook
I will never open again.

This is a poem in thanks for the songs
that creep into my periphery,
that make me stop and move slowly for the pen
in case they scare and scatter.

The melodies that suddenly crash to life
when I trip over the right chord
and place it beneath them
and wonder how they were ever apart.

The choruses that elude me
leaving a verse,
open ended like a raw wound,
but give me something to come back to,
the net of something half done
when I cannot bear the white page of something new.

This poem is a thank you to all the paintings
that come together slowly
after several hundred deliberate marks,
join one another
and steady my hand,
while a radio chatters background in the oil wet room.

For each brick, on a drawing of a building
that takes my mind on a long walk
and lets it imagine what caused that hole
on the pale wooden siding
on an imaginary house
that, for that moment, is so real I could live in it.

Also for the loose lines and coarse marks
I scrub onto scrap sheets
on a messy floor,
alert to the urgency,
with paint on my fingers and arms
that I get to wash off before bed.

The time machine lines
sketched out in a small book,
on a long train,
that make the other passengers disappear
until I reach my destination
and leave the thing half done.

This is a thank you
to all the words,
notes,
and guitar strings
that take me from one end of a blank white page to the other,
in one piece,
somewhat sane,
with something left behind me.

Advice for Aspiring Artists

Stop feeling sorry for yourself.
Eat well.
Don't watch television just before bed.
Wash your hands before dinner.
Don't run with sharp objects facing toward you.
Wear your seatbelt.
Always fasten your mask before attending to your child's.
Look both ways before crossing the street.
Don't turn your back on a bear.
Don't worry if you haven't found 'The One' yet.
Don't drive angry.
Stop, drop and roll.
Go easy.
Go to sleep.
Go make something for fuck's sake.

Cigarette Song

Dear smoking,
I used you as a tool
to escape loud parties,
just you and I in the cool night sky,
not talking to strangers.
And if someone ever joined us outside
that's where the best conversations always lived.

We would wait for buses and trains together,
the time going faster with you by my side.
And the outside early rise,
when I couldn't tell the smoke from you,
from the steam of my breath in the morning air.

After long-haul flights,
while others ran into the sign holding arms of loved ones,
it was you I steadfast ran to,
in the warm outside climate, beside an airport ashtray
we were reunited like lovers.

After sex I would reach for you,
the errant cliché.
And in hospital car parks,
like final goodbyes
in case they took you away from me.

When an idea or verse had come to me
and I had spent an ardent day putting it down,
it was you who heard it first
as we sat at the window listening back,
letting the air in,
both catching my breath.

During my time on the ward,
the smoking area was like a vacation
I would take every half an hour,
rain or shine,
a reason to get out of bed.

And I still remember when we first met,
the honeymoon phase,
sneaking away to steal moments,
after school and with friends in the night.
I remember the post-show excuse for no encore.
The long drives.
The thinking stick.

And now, after all we've been through,
I've given up on you.
Farewell old slow-suicide friend,
I'm breathing.

Telegram for a Sleepless Fool

Stop.
Do not breathe deeply
Pass lovingly
Onto somewhere clean
Stop.
Damn it kid
Don't look at me like I'm something to bleed on
For fear of staining surfaces
Or leaving fingerprints
Stop.
Hellfire darling,
You're something
With your dress hiked up round your gun belt
Heart in your mouth
Bent over laughing
Suddenly aware of your hands
Stop.
Don't start with me
I'm too tired for armoury fights
Too tired
Too too tired
And if you ever need someone to need you
Don't come crying to me.
When the buck stops at dancing
And you're suddenly screaming
And your eyes feel like you stole them
And you're running like a scissor kick
And your toes dig in for impact
And your gums bleed for someone to feed them
Your arms
Get tired
Of typing
So stop.

And that faint sound of laughter in your head
When autocorrect guesses the next word in your poem
In one of those 4 a.m. writing-on-phones affairs
When you wonder if a keypad
Could write all the teeth and blood of you
Without your hands to tell it
What your human heart is feeling
Stop.
I'm low
Like the sun in the evening
Or the sudden you're feeling
Now that the phone lines are cut
And it's dark outside
Without the moon to guide us
And sweetest heart
Don't ask me where I get my chords
Or how I come to feeling
When I have spent my days senseless
Like an animal
In an open field
Looking desperately for fences
Stop.
We must sleep surely
Before the sun brings me coffee and daytime TV
And tells me it's all I've been wanting
When we both know I only drink tea
Because my heart is set to 'burglary'
From the moment I wake
To the moment I dream
And I don't watch TV
For fear of the sea
And coming to my senses
Stop.

The Bedless Horseman

You are not an ending dearest heart,
though the days may close around you
and your arms may draw the night sky
like a vast curtain,
you are a starting again.
Every morning that your eyes lift their lids,
you are a reminder that there is more yet to do
until the breath of my chest leaves me.

And now, while travelling for work,
I cannot remember the day ahead of me
and shudder awake,
with no skinny arms to catch me,
and make morning jokes
about badly written dreams.
It is more violent than a horsehead,
the lack of you,
languid and thick with shaken sleep
the Great Canadian Love of My Life.

Ode to a London Apartment

Darling tiny southwest London flat,
you are where I made myself,
your cold Victorian walls kept close around me,
your door mostly shut
to keep out the warm.

We spent eight long years
building forts together,
as you watched my hands
make art and dinner daily.

You have diligently sheltered me
on frosty winter mornings
so I could sit at the open window
watching steam from my tea leave the house.

    *

I made my first record in you
literally, sat at your newly laid floors,
cutting CD sleeves from card until my fingers bled
and stamping my name on the front.

We sent them outside to be listened to,
so hopeless and resigned,
both shocked to find
that they landed and gave me a job.

I made my fifth inside you too,
remember how I crammed string players
into your tiny bedroom
to perch upon borrowed chairs.

And there was the time
that a song came to me, like an old friend,
while parakeets gathered
to hear it on the tree outside the window.

*

Several brilliant women
have made it past your door,
to laugh with me till sunrise
and arch their wild spines on the bed,

their naked shadows cast across your walls
while they walk from bedroom to bathroom,
only you could see me then,
looking like an actor during interval.

*

You are where I lost myself,
crumbled in your brickwork,
clawing at your cornices
to stop myself from falling.

And now when I come to your door,
all I can think of is lying
shuddering on your bathroom floor,
my eyes like Catherine wheels.

The hours I spent
unable to leave the frigid bedframe,
staring at your dirty ceilings
boiling from the inside out,

While you let water in
from your mangled roof,
like some Marlovian traitor,
to fall on my pillow of all places.

*

But now, somewhat found,
as I pack my belongings and leave,
I don't much like to think
of strangers moving theirs in,

Unaware of the hours we spent
with paint on both our skin,
songs made of longing
ringing through the hall.

Or what you've seen in me,
the way we would sit quietly
at pre-dawn windows,
listening to foxes in the dark.

But, such is the way with homes,
and I'm sure I feel no different
to the early Victorian inhabitant,
who hated the thought of some artist

Two hundred years in the future,
with unwashed hair
and a laptop,
writing songs on your living room floor.

On the Train to Attend the First Death of My Father

How these kinds of crises
are always surrounded
by the silent comfort of friends
and hastily made sandwiches
wrapped in tin foil

and train rides
where you know you are racing to get there
but cannot help the helplessness
of sitting down to do so
with tea in paper cups

and there are always waiting rooms
that stop your running feet
and make you sit
next to strangers also in crisis
with tea again
at your shaking lips.

By Blood

I have carried my brother to hell and back
and he has carried me
and we are both heavy,
we both wear our smiles like straitjackets
to stop us from lashing out.
We have long conversations
about why the family won't grow the fuck up
and how long a piece of string can be
and throwing pets in the trash.

Close Calls

Thus far I have avoided
the glistening edge of a blade,
becoming distracted, by the finish of its wooden handle
the weight of its mass
and the name of its maker
wondering how he lives.

The soft release of pills
has never managed to find me,
saved by the fact they get stuck in my throat
and a hate of bitter casings
and fear of the small print
hiding side effects.

I have kept a safe distance
from the sweet release of petrol fumes
by avoiding gas stations,
staying in the car,
checking my phone,
and shouting snack requests through the window.

Rope has eluded my neck,
my attention diverted by its snake-dance,
my father's fear of indoor heights
(anecdotally inherited),
and, in spite of a short stint as boyscout,
an inability to tie knots.

And I have escaped the edge of buildings
for thirty tired years,
due to a distinct notion
that I couldn't bear my final feeling
being a deep disappointment
at not being able to fly.

Alarm

I am the gloaming dark,
a pale white hand from an earthy cloak,
a raven's song
in a threadbare tree
that sounds a lot like 'leave me'.

I am a hole in the fence
at the end of the garden,
where you just know an eye will appear.
I'm a rusted blade,
held by a man
whose name you don't know,
but folks all say is new in town.

I am telephone wires
making whirring sounds
in a quiet street
in October.
I am bedsheets on a washing line
making shadows on your wall.
A painting of someone else's relatives
with the eyes cut out
and a broken frame,
in an attic you speed-walk to leave.

I am a leaning tree
and a curtain in the breeze
caught by torchlight and mistaken for fleeing the scene.

I am the sickly sweet, plastic smell
of rubber Halloween masks
and the sound of your breathing within them.

I am fingernails on doorframes.
I am a scarecrow failing his post,
a door creak,
a bat wing,
a childless swing,
I'm piano strings,
I am whistling winds,
the middle of the night,
I am a terribly frightening thing,
believe me,
if you look at me right.

Magpie

I wondered if bad luck would follow
the day the magpie looked so guilty
when you asked him where his wife was
and why he had a shovel
and if that was blood on his wing.

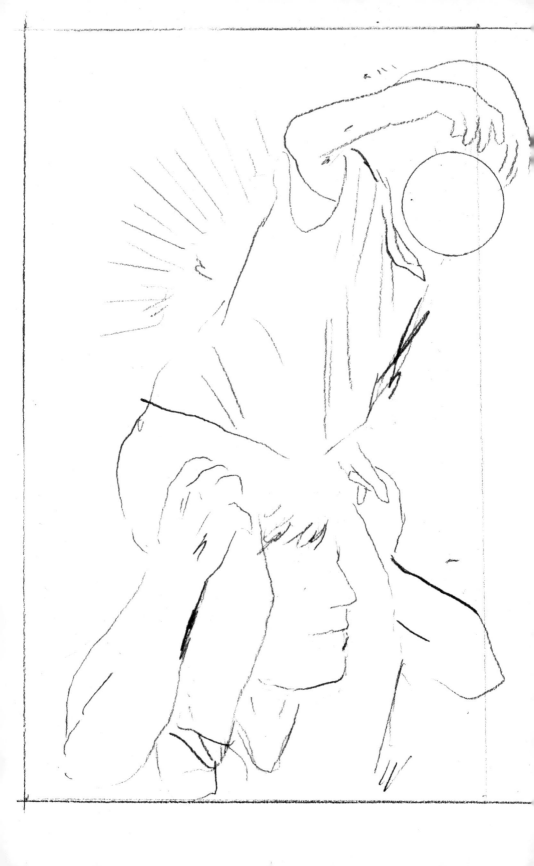

And When He Is Gone

And when he is gone
I will wonder where his mind is
without a brain to make it so,
where his loud laugh now rings out
without living lungs to carry it.

And when he has left us
I will search the night sky for his stories
and wonder which stars are his twinkling eyes.
I will look for him in houses
where we once sat comfortably,
finishing each other's crosswords.

And when we are without him
the world will seem too quiet,
the house I grew up in
will echo with want of him
and I will not like to go there
for fear of seeing a space
ripped out of the world
in his silhouette,
head back laughing.

Chopping Wood in November

I am reminded, on this bitter chill day,
with each pendulous swing of the axe,
that there is a fire to be built back indoors.

The handle recedes softly through my palm
as the waiting blade descends
and meets its many-ringed foe;

the log, that tears itself in two,
as though the halves
have been desperate to be apart

and release that musk of fresh wood,
unopen to the elements,
for all its growing years;

cedar scent,
oak balm,
bark dust.

And the satisfaction of the blade
getting wedged in the block
is heavenly distracting.

The splinters in my icy hands
so unnoticed go
as I clear the halves inside,

and ready to set them alight.
the city is a distant dream.
Thank god for firewood.

For Danielle

She is the most fragile suit of armour I have ever worn
but she keeps the wounds away
better than any inch-thick, tempered-iron breastplate, kid.

Sometimes when she speaks I hear the world get born,
our savage, fumbled history stretching out behind us;
the wars fought for scraps of land,
the gods invented,
paths worn,
roads built,
all so she could tell me how her day was,
in a voice as thin as ivy,
through lips I could have drawn.

Her smile makes you feel like a carnival prize,
the presence of kindness,
who talks to birds like friends,
and loves the sound of voices
in spite of what they say.

I love her to the joints of her fingers and grin
every time she looks at me
like I am worth the days I wake to.

Some unthinking mornings
I forget she is my floorboards
and sit alone dreaming up a life outside her walls,
until she rounds the corner waving
with sleep stuck in her eyes
and I kick myself for thinking
I was ever anything without her
and life was worth singing for
before she gave me words.

She is the greatest apology the world has ever offered
for the aridity of its deserts,
and the bitter of its rain,
a calm reminder I can stand up,
even when I can't.
I know she'll get me upright
she's in the business of miracles.

She is the blade of grass you missed
when you were staring at an orchid,
that took all the sun, sea and music of the world,
and, made substance, came bursting forth,
to sit quietly, unnoticed in the soil
watching others have their days.
But she could take down a redwood
with one 'good morning sweetheart'
and shrug the leaves away.

When she plays guitar
each fumbled note sings more elegance
than any pure resonance that I have ever heard.
When she sings I hear her childhood come pouring out
and think of lakes
and fishing
and snow.

She is my arm,
the one I write with,
and hold close while I'm sleeping.
The right hand,
the high notes,
the day.

And if I am ever gone away
with no chance of returning,
take her gently in your story
and lift her from harm and hellfire
to a quiet place,
careful though stranger
she is stronger than she looks.

Ghost Story

The ghost was not the phone call, through quiet sobs
telling me he had passed
softly in the night.

It was not the look in my brother's eyes as I arrived
at the cheap hotel
conveniently near the hospital.

Nor was the ghost
the quiet of the car rides
from one white building to another.

It wasn't the smile of the nurses
now familiar with our faces
as I mumbled 'I'm here for his wallet'
with exhausted eyes.

And it may be a surprise to learn
that the ghost was not the silence of his room
or the indentation in his shape
still left in the hospital bed,

his keys and reading glasses
organised like a still life on his bedside table
or the pile of books I had given him
roughly thumbed and put aside.

The ghost I found, which took the very breath from me
in that magnolia room
while searching for the wallet

was my hands in his coat pockets
where the only other hands to enter
had been his.

The ghost was old receipts
softened over time
by his large rough hands
on winter days walking through town.

My thin fingers
in the imprint of his
comfortably wrought in the fabric
of the only coat he ever wore
tattered at the elbows.

This was the phantom
that had never occurred to me
until I felt it
in the eternal stillness of that room
a bird singing, outside the window
as if asking where his friend was today.

An Afternoon of Not Much at All

I ascend a creaking staircase
with a fresh tea in my hands,
which are still brown and chalked with wood dust
from chopping logs all morning,
still buoyed by the worn axe handle,
the reassuring weight of its head.

My feet now bare on warm carpet
climb comfortably up
to where they both know a piano sits,
waiting for my fingers
to perform a more menial task
and see what notes fall out.

I am unburdened by the fact
that the silence is littered with birdsong,
allowing any halting in my playing
to sound more beautiful than anything I might write.
The keys attend my fingertips,
as dust motes hang in sunbeams.

The Raeburn gurgles familiarly
from the kitchen downstairs,
and between two particular chords
in the key of not-thinking,
a horse whinnies displeasure
at being walked past the house.

And while plucking a worn-out arpeggio
from the aged strings of the instrument
the warm air swirls around me
and I turn to the door
descend the soft steps
and walk in the woods until dinner.

VII
For Now

Good Night

I write this from where I live,
a wild house on the South Downs
with nothing but trees, molehills and long grass
for as far as I can see,
and I can see pretty far.

No longer is my vision stunted, by loosely hung buildings
stacked on top of themselves, clawing at each other for air,
the feral grass that scents my morning
has never known the cruel sting of a mower's blades,
the trees' limbs that creak at my rattling window
moan ancient good evenings
that sing me to sleep.

When I am cold I light a fire,
when I am hot I open windows,
and let England's breeze fan me cool.
And now when my brain turns to fits and shivers,
as it is so wont to do,
I think of how the birds must feel,
with buckshot around every corner
waiting to pick them from the sky.

And when it gets too much I drive
past farms and forests
to another such wild place,
or the ocean,
or a nearby cottage,
to sit among voices in a kitchen filled with friends.
Work is no longer a desperate escape,
a gasping for distraction,
but a pleasure.
I'm fine,

thanks for asking.

Keaton Henson is a musician, poet and visual artist from England.
He has released seven studio albums, three books and held several
exhibitions. He also composes for orchestra.
He enjoys doing the things mentioned above and being left alone.